AGE 9-10
Year 5

Maths and English
Year 5 Optional Tests

Acknowledgements

The authors and publisher would like to thank the following for permission to reproduce material in this book.

gil's Saga and *The Head Ransom*, adapted from texts by Magnus Magnusson

he Jorvik Viking Centre, adapted from the Jorvik Viking Centre website.

very effort has been made to trace and acknowledge ownership of opyright material but if any have been inadvertently overlooked, the ublisher will be pleased to make the necessary alterations at the first pportunity.

irst published 2001
xclusively for WHSmith by

lodder & Stoughton Educational,
 division of Hodder Headline Ltd
38 Euston Road
ondon NW1 3BH

ext and illustrations © Hodder & Stoughton Educational 2001

ll rights reserved. No part of this publication may be reproduced or ransmitted in any form or by any means, electronic or mechanical, ncluding photocopying, recording or any information storage and retrieval ystem, without permission in writing from the publisher.

 CIP record for this book is available from the British Library.

uthors: Steve Mills and Hilary Koll (Maths);
hristine Moorcroft and Ray Barker (English)

SBN 0340 84601 1

rinted and bound by Graphycems, Spain.

NOTE: The tests, questions and advice in this book are not reproductions of the official test materials sent to schools. The official testing process is supported by guidance and training for teachers in setting and marking tests and interpreting the results. The results achieved in the tests in this book may not be the same as are achieved in the official tests.

Contents	Page
Introduction	
The National Tests: A Summary	ii
Maths Test	
Maths at Year 5	1
Maths Test Part A	2
Maths Test Part B	14
Mental Maths Test	19
Maths Test Answers	22
National Curriculum Levels	27
English Test	
English at Year 5	28
Reading Test	29
Writing Test	44
Spelling Test	52
Handwriting Test	54
English Test Answers	56
National Curriculum Levels	62

Introduction

The National Tests: A Summary

What are the National Tests?
Children who attend state schools in England and Wales sit National Tests (also known as SATs) at the ages of 7, 11 and 14, usually at the beginning of May. They may also sit optional tests in the intervening years – many schools have chosen to adopt these tests. The test results are accompanied by an assessment by the child's teacher (at Key Stage 3 this also covers non-tested subjects such as History or Geography).

The results are used by the school to assess each child's level of knowledge and progress in English and Maths at Key Stage 1 and English, Maths and Science at Key Stages 2 and 3. They also provide useful guidance for the child's next teacher when he or she is planning the year's work.

The educational calendar for children aged 5–14 is structured as follows:

Key Stage	Year	Age by end of year	National Test
1 (KS1)	1	6	
	2	7	KEY STAGE 1
2 (KS2)	3	8	Optional Year 3
	4	9	Optional Year 4
	5	10	Optional Year 5
	6	11	KEY STAGE 2
3 (KS3)	7	12	
	8	13	
	9	14	KEY STAGE 3

Test timetable
The Key Stage 1 National Tests are carried out in **May**. They often form part of children's normal school day, as they are generally practical and teacher-assessed. Many children at Key Stage 1 do not even realise they are taking a test.

Key Stage 2 tests take place in one week in May. All children sit the same test at the same time. In 2002, the tests will take place in the week of **13–17 May**. Your child's school will be able to provide you with a detailed timetable.

Key Stage 3 students will sit their tests on **7–13 May**.

Levels
National average levels have been set for children's results in the National Tests. The levels are as follows:

LEVEL	AGE 7 (Key Stage 1)	AGE 11 (Key Stage 2)	AGE 14 (Key Stage 3)
8			
7			
6			
5			
4			
3			
2			
2a			
2b			
2c			
1			

- BELOW EXPECTED LEVEL
- EXPECTED LEVEL
- ABOVE EXPECTED LEVEL
- EXCEPTIONAL

Results
Your child's school will send you a report indicating his or her levels in the tests and the teacher assessment.

The school's overall test results will be included in local and national league tables, which are published in most newspapers.

What can parents do to help?
While it is never a good idea to encourage cramming, you can help your child to succeed by:

- Making sure he or she has enough food, sleep and leisure time during the test period.
- Practising important skills such as writing and reading stories, spelling and mental arithmetic.
- Telling him or her what to expect in the test, such as important symbols and key words.
- Helping him or her to be comfortable in test conditions including working within a time limit, reading questions carefully and understanding different ways of answering.

Maths

Maths at Year 5

Typical 7 year-olds attain Level 2 in maths at the end of Year 2. By the end of Year 5 most children will be working towards Level 4. Some might be attaining a Level 4.

Setting the test

The written test

Allow between 45 minutes and one hour to complete the written test. If your child attempts Part B, allow longer.

Your child will need a ruler, pencil, rubber and, if possible, a small mirror or piece of tracing paper. No extra writing paper is needed. The use of a calculator is not permitted.

The written test is split into two parts, A and B. If your child scores highly in Part A, he or she can go on to try the harder questions in Part B. There is not a strict time limit on this test, but do not force your child to continue if he or she can no longer answer any questions.

If your child has difficulty in reading the questions, these can be read aloud, provided the mathematical words are not altered or explained. Where necessary, children can dictate their answers for you to write them down. For large numbers, however, a child should be clear which digits are intended to be written, e.g. for a number such as three thousand and six the child must indicate that this should be written three, zero, zero, six.

The mental test

The marks scored on the mental mathematics test are not included when levelling at Year 5. However, in the Year 6 National Test your child's mental scores will form part of the overall mark used for levelling.

The mental test should take approximately 10–15 minutes to give, and it is necessary for you to read aloud the questions on page **19**, which you could copy for this purpose. Your child will only need a pencil and rubber for the mental test.

The mental test contains a series of questions for you to read to your child and answer sheets for him or her to write answers on. Allow only the time suggested for each question and read each question twice.

Marking the test

Next to each question is a number indicating how many marks the question or part of the question is worth. Enter your child's mark into the circle, using the answer pages to help you decide how many points to award.

Find your child's total score from the written test and refer to page 27 for information about the level your child might be working at.

Maths Test
Part A

1 Use all of these digits to make a **three-digit number smaller than 390.**

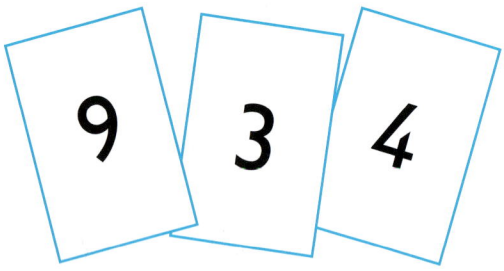 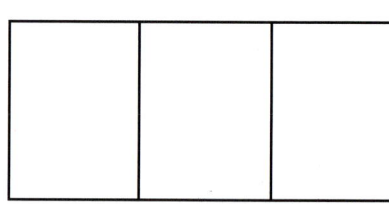

Write the number you have made in words.

_____

_____

2 The **sum** of the digits of **one** of these telephone numbers is **27**. Whose number is it?

Theresa
020 7456 7243

Ling
07990 174593

Jackie
01941 352 5311

Ingrid
0117 2525112

TOTAL
2

2

Maths Test Part A

3 Draw a line to join the answers with the matching questions.

26	68 + 14
42	14 x 3
57	6 x 6
36	100 – 74
82	(20 x 3) – 1
59	28 + 29

2

4 Fill in the missing numbers in these sequences.

1 4 9 ◯ 25 ◯

3 6 12 ◯ ◯ 96

1

1

TOTAL

4

Maths Test Part A

5 This is a diagram to show the number of children who have pets in Class 5.

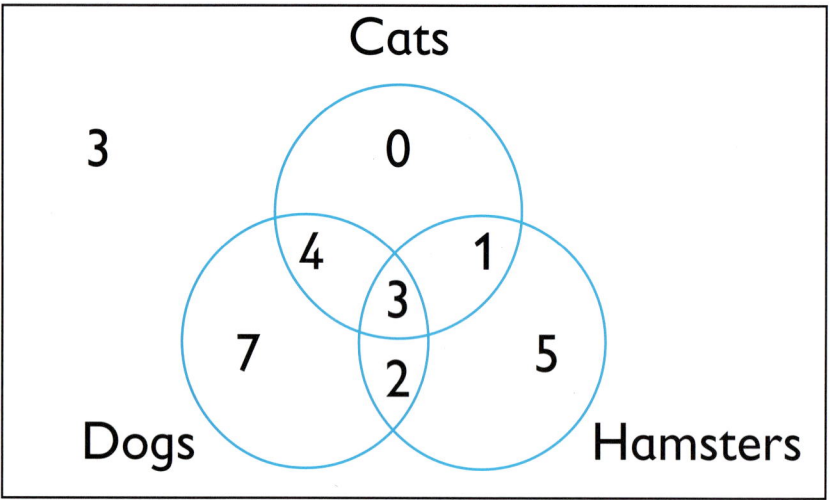

How many children have a cat **and** a dog but no hamster?

How many children have **only** a hamster?

How many children do **not** have a cat, a dog or a hamster?

6 Finish this sentence.

A quadrilateral with equal sides and equal angles is called a ....

7 Draw **all** the **lines of symmetry** onto each of the badges below. You can use a mirror or tracing paper.

2

Badge A

Badge B

Badge C

TOTAL

2

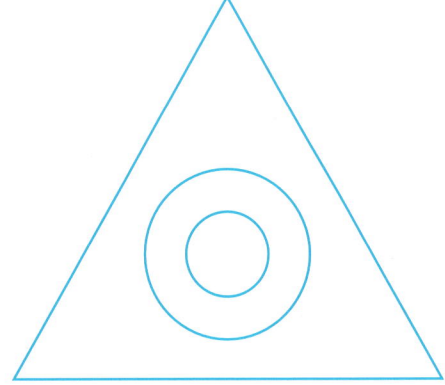

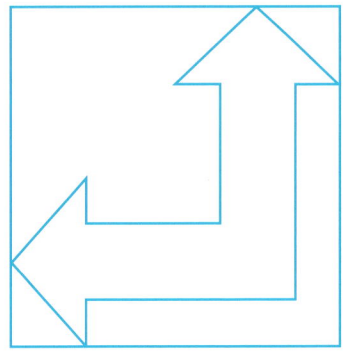

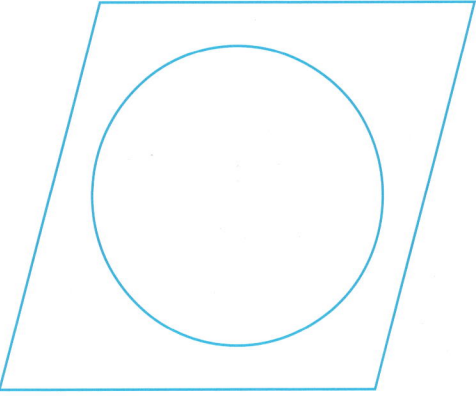

Maths Test Part A

8 Draw a ring around **all** the numbers that when divided by **5** have a **remainder of 3**.

11   25   23   26
32   47   14   18

9 Find the area of Shape A.

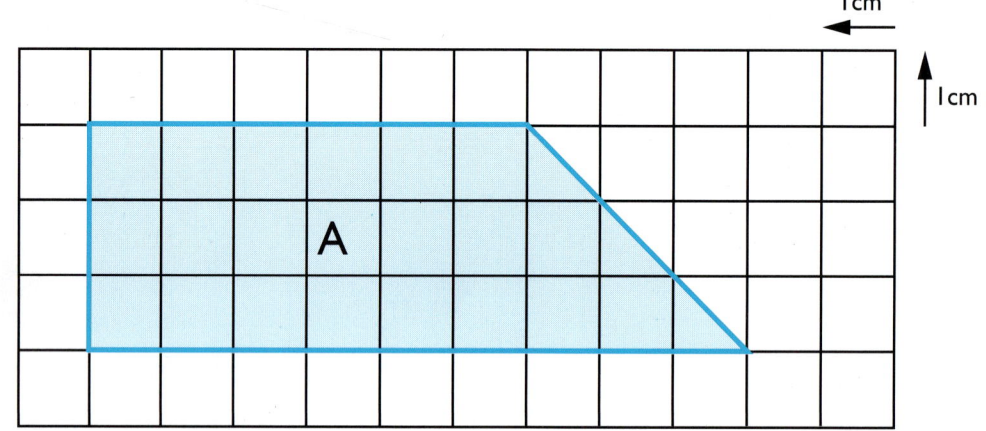

Area of Shape A = ▢ cm²

10 A shop sells doughnuts in boxes of 4. How many doughnuts are there in 64 boxes?

TOTAL 3

11 This graph shows the journeys a lift made during half an hour. The lift travelled from the ground floor up to floor 7.

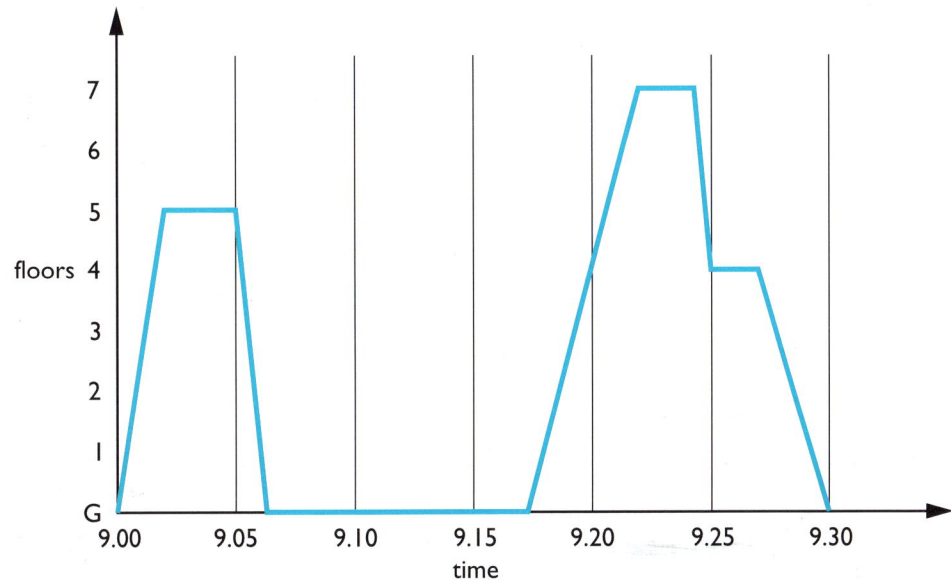

Estimate how many minutes the lift stayed at floor 5.

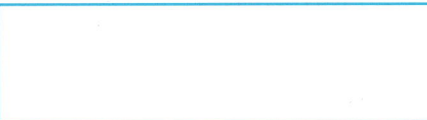

minutes

1

Where was the lift at 9.26?

1

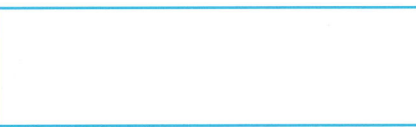

Estimate the time (to the nearest minute) that the lift reached floor 7.

1

TOTAL

3

Maths Test Part A

12 Tick the picture below that is **not** a picture of a type of prism.

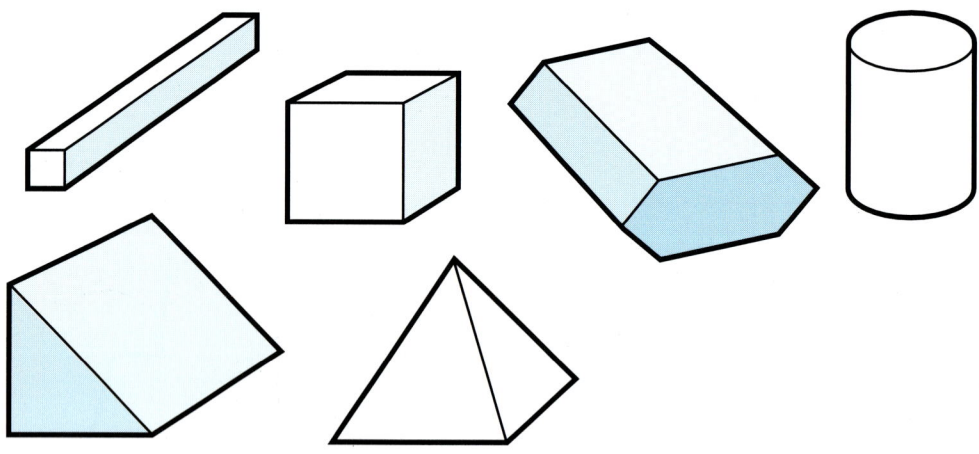

13 In your own words, explain what a square number is.

_____
_____
_____
_____

14 Fill in the missing numbers in the circles.

74 − ◯ = 28

◯ + 39 = 56

Maths Test Part A

15 What fraction of this group of rabbits is grey?

1

16 Draw a tick inside the shape that has **fewer than four sides, reflective symmetry** and **one right angle.**

1

TOTAL

2

Maths Test Part A

17 Sean has exactly **£2.65** in **5p** coins in his money box.

How many 5p coins does he have?

18 This kettle has a capacity of 2 litres. The ball indicates how much water is in the kettle.

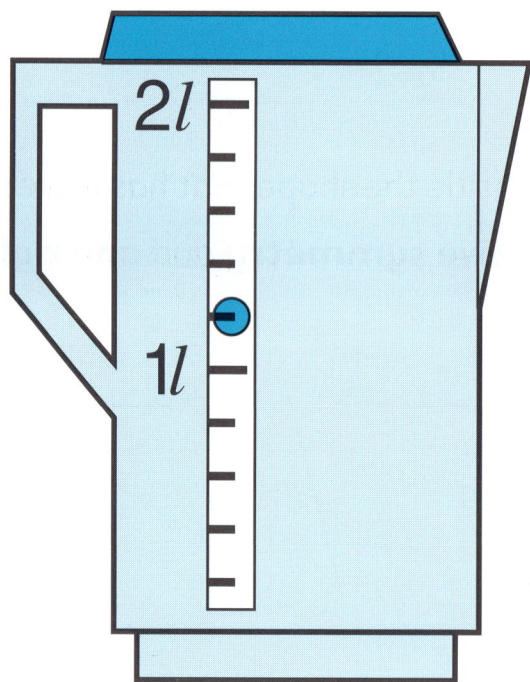

How many millilitres of water would it take to fill the kettle to the 2 litre mark?

ml

19 Draw arrows to complete this diagram.

The arrows stand for:

→

'rounded to the nearest whole number is…'

6.9	5
6.21	
5 1/4	6
7 7/8	
6.09	7
7.48	
5 9/10	8

(Arrow drawn from 6.9 to 7)

Maths Test Part A

20 When this spinner is spun, the probability of it landing on the number 1 is **one half.** The probability of it landing on the number 2 is also **one half.**

The spinner is spun a **first time** and lands on the number **2**. It is now spun a **second time**.

Put a cross on the line to show the probability of the spinner landing on the number **2** on the **second spin**.

0   1/4   1/2   3/4   1

21 This triangle has a perimeter of 30 cm.

Use a ruler to draw a rectangle with a perimeter of 44 cm.

STOP HERE AND MARK THIS TEST

Maths Test
Part B

22 Mr Smith works for 'The Fix-it Firm'.

He earns exactly **£500 per month**.

How much does he earn in **one year**?

The firm gives him a pay rise. He now earns **15%** more.

How much does he now earn **each month**?

23 These prices were scanned into a shop till.

£5.63   £4.65   £8.98

£10.10   £9.07

Find the total of these prices.

Maths Test Part B

24 Zahir counts the number of times he can kick a ball in the air without it falling to the ground. He has tried this seven times.

These are his results:

12, 16, 11, 17,
20,   3, 20

What is the **median** of these numbers?

1

25 On a dartboard there are **10** equal sections numbered from 1 to 10.

A dart lands in one of these sections.
Circle the fraction that shows the probability of it landing in a section numbered **less than 5**.

$\frac{1}{10}$ $\frac{4}{5}$ $\frac{5}{10}$ $\frac{10}{1}$ $\frac{6}{5}$ $\frac{4}{10}$

1

TOTAL

2

Maths Test Part B

26 Here are some models, made from centimetre cubes, which form a pattern.

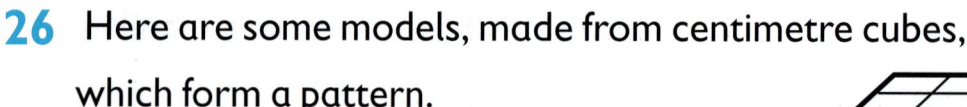

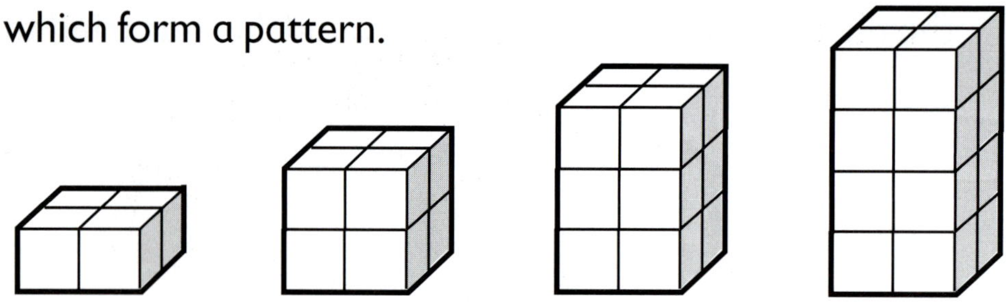

The relationship between the number of cubes and the height of the model can be written as:

The height of the model = the number of cubes ÷ 4

How many cubes are there in a model which has a height of 12 cm?

27 What numbers are the arrows pointing to?

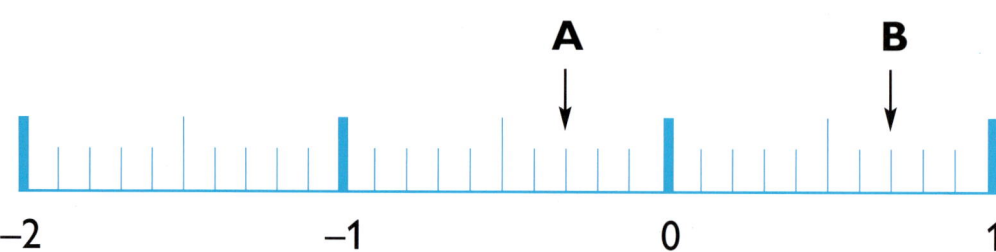

A =

B =

Maths Test Part B

28 A car uses approximately **1 litre** of petrol to travel **8 miles.**

About how many litres of petrol does it use to travel **72 miles?**

Peter went on a journey in this car. He used **13 litres** of petrol. How many miles did he travel?

29 Javed watched TV between these two times.

16:35   **19:25**

For how long did he watch TV?

| hours | minutes |

Maths Test Part B

30 Charlotte goes on a **3 kilometre** run.

Each pace she takes is **60 cm**.

How many paces does she take?

31 $3x + 5 =$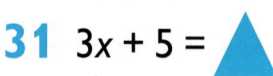

If *x* is 4, what is the value of the triangle?

32 Fill in the missing numbers.

36.74 ÷ 100 =

58.6 − 4.52 =

Mental Maths Test
Questions

"For this first set of questions you have five seconds to work out each answer and write it down."

1. What is half of one hundred and four?
2. What is seven multiplied by eight?
3. Write the number six thousand and nine in figures.
4. What is fifty per cent of eighty grams?
5. A train journey begins at two thirty five. It ends at three fifteen. How long does the journey last?
6. There are one hundred and twelve marbles in a jar. Seventy five are red and the rest are blue. How many are blue?
7. Add seven and a half metres to three and a half metres.
8. What is ten more than one thousand one hundred and ninety five?
9. The temperature was six degrees and is now minus three degrees. By how much has the temperature fallen?
10. Look at the answer sheet. Which number is the arrow pointing to?
11. Six children share three pounds equally between them. How much does each child get?
12. Write two numbers that add up to seven and a half.

"For the next set of questions you have ten seconds to work out each answer and write it down."

13. How many grams are there in one and a half kilograms?
14. Look at the answer sheet. What is the median of these numbers?
15. What is the probability of rolling an even number on an ordinary dice?
16. What is the cost of five T-shirts at three pounds ninety nine pence each?
17. What number is half way between five point one and five point two?
18. Look at the drawing on the answer sheet. What will the shape look like when it is reflected in the mirror line? Shade the correct shape.
19. I'm thinking of a number. I double it and then subtract two. My answer is thirty. What is my number?
20. A clock shows eleven o'clock. What is the angle between the two hands?

Mental Maths Test
Answer Sheet

5-second questions

1.
2.
3.
4. _____ grams | 50% 80 grams
5. _____ minutes | 2:35 3:15
6. _____ | 112 75 red
7. _____ metres
8.
9. _____ degrees
10. _____ | 20 30 40
11. _____ pence
12.

TOTAL 12

Mental Maths Test

10-second questions

13. _____ grams

14. | | 6   8 |
    | | 8 |
    | | 3   5 |

15.

16. £ _____   5   £3.99

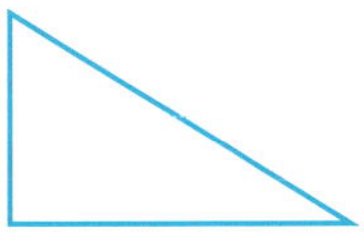

17.

18. _____ mirror line

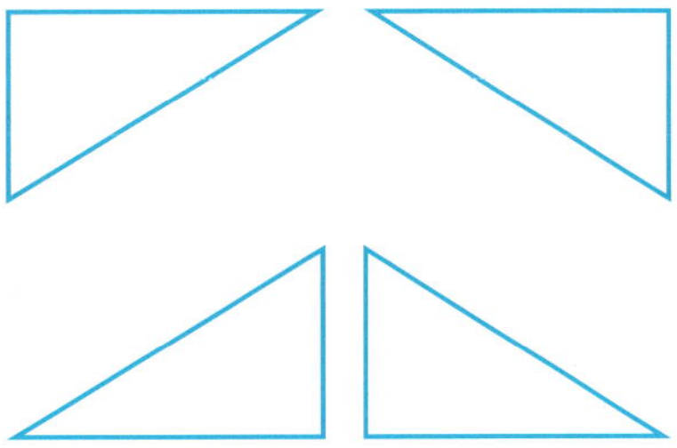

19.

20.

Answers
Maths Test

Question number	Answer	Mark	Parent's notes and additional information
Part A			
1	349 and *'three hundred and forty nine'*.	1	Accept incorrect spellings where the intention is clear, e.g. 'hunded' or 'fourty'
2	Ingrid	1	
3	26 = 100 − 74 42 = 14 x 3 57 = 28 + 29 36 = 6 x 6 82 = 68 + 14 59 = (20 x 3) − 1 Award one mark if all but two matches are correct.	2	
4a	1, 4, 9, **16**, 25, **36** Both must be correct for a point to be awarded.	1	Children should recognise that these are square numbers. A square number is a number that is made from multiplying another number by itself, e.g. 1 = 1 x 1, 4 = 2 x 2, 9 = 3 x 3… etc. Children should learn the square numbers to 100, i.e. 1, 4, 9, 16, 25, 36, 49, 64, 81, 100.
4b	3, 6, 12, **24, 48**, 96	1	Children should notice that this is a doubling pattern.
5a	4	1	
5b	5	1	
5a	3	1	
6	square	1	A quadrilateral is a 2-dimensional shape with four straight sides. The only shape with four equal sides and four equal angles is a square.
7	Award 1 mark if only two badges are correctly marked.	2	**Three** lines should be marked on badge A, in the places shown. **One** only should be marked on Badge B and **two** on Badge C. A mirror or tracing paper can be used for this question.

22

Maths Test Answers

Question number	Answer	Mark	Parent's notes and additional information
8	23, 18 Only these two should be ringed.	1	Children should recognise patterns in the remainders created by dividing by 5, e.g. 12, 17, 22, 27... all have a remainder of 2 when divided by 5. Similarly, 13, 18, 23, 28... have remainders of 3.
9	$22\frac{1}{2}$ cm² or 22.5 cm²	1	Areas of shapes can be found by counting the number of squares (including part squares) inside the shape. Alternatively, this shape can be broken into a rectangle (6 squares by 3 squares = 18 squares) and a triangle that is half the area of a 3 x 3 square.
10	256	1	Children might incorrectly give the answer 16 by dividing rather than multiplying by 4.
11a	3 minutes	1	
11b	Floor 4	1	
11c	9.22	1	
12	The pyramid should be ticked.	1	A prism is a shape with the same cross section along its length. It has two identical faces at either end.
13	An explanation that includes reference to numbers such as 1, 4, 9, 16, 25, and/or an explanation of multiplying a number by itself to create a square number, and/or the suggestion that these numbers of dots can be arranged to form a square, e.g.	1	A square number is a number that is made from multiplying another number by itself, e.g. $1 = 1 \times 1$, $4 = 2 \times 2$, $9 = 3 \times 3$ Children should learn the square numbers to 100, i.e. 1, 4, 9, 16, 25, 36, 49, 64, 81, 100.
14a	74 − 46 = 28	1	

23

Maths Test Answers

Question number	Answer	Mark	Parent's notes and additional information
14b	**17** + 39 = 56	1	Some children may make the mistake of adding 39 and 56. Children need to realise that despite having an addition sign, this question can be answered by subtracting 39 from 56.
15	$\frac{2}{5}$	1	
16	(triangle)	1	Each of the other shapes does not meet the description in at least one way.
17	53	1	Any non-calculator method can be used to find the answer.
18	800 ml	1	Children need to know that there are 1000 ml in one litre.
19	6.21 → 6 $5\frac{1}{4}$ → 5 $7\frac{7}{8}$ → 8 6.09 → 6 7.48 → 7 $5\frac{9}{10}$ → 6 Award two marks for all correct. If at least four of the six are correctly joined, award one mark.	2	
20	$\frac{1}{2}$	1	Children can often become confused with probability questions of this type. Just because a result has occurred once, it is no less likely to happen again the next time. On the second spin there is still a one in two chance of scoring a 2, so the probability must be one half.
21	A rectangle with the length and the width totalling 22 cm, e.g. 10 cm and 12 cm or 11 cm and 11 cm etc. The angles should be right angles.	1	The perimeter is the distance all the way around the shape. If the perimeter is 44 cm, then the total of the four sides is 44 cm.

Maths Test Answers

Question number	Answer	Mark	Parent's notes and additional information
Part B			
22a	£6000	1	Any non-calculator method is acceptable.
22b	£575	1	To find 15% of £500, children can first find 15% of £100 (=£15) and then multiply this by 5 to find 15% of 500. Alternatively, this can be viewed as $\frac{15}{100}$ × 500 or 15 ÷ 100 × 500.
23	£38.43	1	Any non-calculator method is acceptable.
24	16	1	To find the median, the numbers must be ordered. Once ordered, the median value is the number in the middle of the list, e.g. 3, 11, 12, **16**, 17, 20, 20,
25	$\frac{4}{10}$	1	The probability of the dart landing in a section numbered 1, 2, 3 or 4 is four out of ten or four tenths.
26	48 cubes	1	A common error that children make with this question is to divide 12 by 4 to give the incorrect answer 3. Show your child that the height is always smaller than the number of cubes used to make the model. So if the height is given as 12 cm, it must take more than 12 centimetre cubes to make it.
27a	A = −0.3	1	
27b	B = 0.7	1	
28a	9 litres	1	72 ÷ 8 = 9
28b	104 miles	1	13 × 8 = 104
29	2 hours 50 minutes	1	If your child has answered 3 hours 10 minutes, show him or her that 3 hours 10 minutes on from 16:35 is 19:45 not 19:25. Javed watches TV for 10 minutes **less** than three hours, not more.
30	5000 paces	1	If each pace is 60 cm, then after 5 paces she has gone 300 cm (3 m). So after 5000 paces she will have travelled 3000 m, which is the same as 3 km. Children need to know that 1000 m = 1 km.
31	17	1	If x stands for the number 4, then three lots of x (three lots of 4) must equal 12. 12 + 5 = 17 so ▲ has the same value as 17.
32a	0.3674	1	
32b	54.08	1	

Answers

Mental Maths Test

1. 52
2. 56
3. 6009
4. 40 g
5. 40 minutes
6. 37
7. 11 m
8. 1205
9. 9 degrees
10. 37
11. 50p
12. Any two numbers that add to make $7\frac{1}{2}$ e.g. $6\frac{1}{2}$ + 1 or 3.2 + 4.3 etc.
13. 1500 g
14. 6
15. $\frac{1}{2}$ or $\frac{3}{6}$
16. £19.95
17. 5.15
18. ▷
19. 16
20. 30°

Award one mark per correct answer.

National Curriculum Levels

Each test has a part A and a part B.

The score is out of a maximum of 45 marks (30 marks for Part A and 15 for part B).

If your child has scored highly in Part A, he or she should go on to try the harder questions in part B.

Write your child's scores below:

Mark scored in Part A

Mark scored in Part B

Total mark

Children at Year 5 might complete a test of this type at school. From this each child can be levelled and graded according to his or her total score. Children do not normally sit a mental maths test at this stage.

Mark	0–10	11 – 15	16 – 20	21 – 25	26 – 30	31 – 35	36 – 39	40–45
Level	Below 3	Level 3C	Level 3B	Level 3A	Level 4C	Level 4B	Level 4A	Level 5

If a child scores very highly on the test, there is a possibility of sitting the Year 6 tests, to gain clearer information about the extent to which he or she is performing at Level 5.

English

English at Year 5

Most children attain Level 3 by the end of Year 4; by the end of year 5 they will be well on the way to Level 4 and may even have attained Level 4. Some might attain Level 5.

You can gain an idea of the level at which your child is working by following the tables on page 62, which show how to convert the marks into a National Curriculum level. No marks are given for writing, but the charts on pages 58 to 60 will help you to judge your child's level of attainment.

Setting the test

Your child will need a pencil and, if possible, a rubber; if you do not have a rubber, ask your child to cross out any mistakes made.

Give your child the tests in the order in which they appear in this book. This is important because the tests are linked by a theme. To understand the Writing Test, your child needs to have read the Reading Test.

No extra paper is needed: the child writes in this book.

Do not ask your child to do all the tests one after the other.

After each test add up your child's marks and use the conversion table on page 62 to work out his or her National Curriculum level.

Reading Test

The Reading Test includes:

- a fiction text
- a poem
- an information text.

The test is designed to assess your child's ability to read, understand and respond to different types of writing.

Presenting the test

It is best to give your child a break between each test.

Allow the following times:

Fiction: 35 minutes
Poetry: 20 minutes
Information: 25 minutes.

At the end of the test, enter his or her mark for each question in the circle provided (the number indicates the possible mark).

The answers are on pages 56 to 57. National Curriculum Levels are given on page 62.

Reading Test

Fiction Reading Test

1. Ask your child to turn to the Fiction Reading Test (page 31).

2. Encourage him or her to read the text carefully.

3. Point out that there are two different types of question: those which give a choice of answers, one of which is ticked, and those which ask for a written answer. Written answers need not be complete sentences.

4. **Do not** help your child to read the rest of the text, although you may help with the spelling of the answers.

5. Ask your child:

   - **to find** the answers in the text, rather than giving answers which he or she already knows;
   - **to tick only one box** to answer each question;
   - **to try** to answer every question;
   - **to leave** any questions he or she **cannot** answer, and go back to them at the end;
   - **to re-read** the text to find the answers to questions.

6. **Allow** your child to read the text **independently** and to answer the questions without any help.

Poetry Reading Test

Repeat the above for the Poetry Reading Test (pages 37 to 39).

Information Reading Test

Repeat the above for the Information Reading Test (pages 40 to 43).

Reading Test
Fiction

From *Egil's Saga*

Egil was restless. He was ready for another sea-voyage. Some years had passed since his raiding expedition to Norway. There had been a furious sea-battle off the coast of Norway, and he had killed Rognvald, the son of King Eirik Bloodaxe, and thirteen of his friends. Eirik declared Egil an outlaw, and his wife, Queen Gunnhild, who was known for her sorcery, put a curse on him.

Egil could not go to Norway – he would be killed at once. But England was surely safe for him – he had fought in a great battle on the side of the king of England, Athelstan: the king owed him a favour. So Egil prepared his ship. In the summer, he left his wife, Asgerd, in charge of their farm at Borg in Iceland, and sailed to England.

He landed on the east coast, not far from York. But he discovered that King Eirik Bloodaxe was there! He had been expelled from Norway and was now king of the Norse people in York. Egil realised that he had no chance of getting away, even in disguise. Someone would recognise him. Besides, he thought it demeaning to be caught trying to run away. So he steeled himself and made up his mind to go to the king.

Egil had a close friend, a Norwegian named Arinbjorn, who was in the service of King Eirik. He went to see Arinbjorn in secret, with some of his crew. Arinbjorn asked him why he had come. Egil told him and said, "Can you give me any help?"

"Did you meet anyone in town who might have recognised you on your way here?" asked Arinbjorn.

"No one," said Egil.

"Then take up your weapons, all of you, and come with me. We must go and see the king," said Arinbjorn.

They set out for the king's residence. The king was sitting at his table. Arinbjorn asked Egil and ten other men to go inside with him.

"Now, Egil," whispered Arinbjorn, "you must offer your head to the king and embrace his foot, and I shall present your case."

They went inside. Arinbjorn went up to the king and greeted him. The king welcomed him and asked what he wanted.

Arinbjorn said, "I have brought here a man who has journeyed a long way to visit you and seek a reconciliation. It is a great honour to you, my lord, when your enemies come to you of their own free will from other lands because they cannot endure your anger even though you are far away. Show this man magnanimity. Make an honourable reconciliation with him for the great honour he does you, by travelling a great distance across difficult seas far from his own home. Nothing but goodwill towards you drove him on this journey."

Reading Test – Fiction

The king looked around and there, over the heads of the other men, he saw the towering figure of Egil. He glared at him and said, "Why are you so foolhardy, Egil, as to dare to come and visit me? We parted in such a manner last time that you could have no hope of my sparing your life."

Then Egil went up to the table and embraced the king's foot, and spoke a verse of greeting. The king replied, "I need not tally the wrongs you have done me. They are so many and so grave that any one of them would be enough to stop you leaving here alive. You have no hope of anything here but death."

Queen Gunnhild said, "Kill Egil – kill him now! Have you forgotten what he has done? Killed your friends and even your own son, and made you a laughing stock. I have never heard of a king and his family being treated so badly."

Arinbjorn said, "If Egil has done the king wrong he can make up for it with a poem of praise which will live for ever."

Gunnhild said, "We do not want to hear his poem of praise. Have Egil taken outside, Eirik, and put to death at once."

"The king must not let himself be told what to do by you . He must not have Egil killed after nightfall: that would be a shameful act."

The king said, "Let it be as you ask, Arinbjorn. Egil shall live tonight. Take him home with you and bring him to me in the morning."

They went up into the loft in Arinbjorn's house and talked things over. Arinbjorn said, "The king was furious, but seemed to calm down a little. Only luck will decide how things will go. Gunnhild will do her best to have you killed. You must stay up all night and compose a poem in praise of Eirik. You can recite it when we go before him in the morning. That is the only way you might save your head."

Arinbjorn left him. He came back at midnight, and asked him how the poem was going. Egil had not composed a line: "A swallow has been sitting at the window twittering all night and I have not had a moment's peace."

Arinbjorn went up through the door which led to the roof, where the bird had been sitting. He saw a strange shape leaving the house. Arinbjorn sat there outside the window all night until dawn, while Egil composed the poem and memorised it. He recited it to Arinbjorn.

"It is time to go to the king" said Arinbjorn.

32

Reading Test – Fiction

1 Egil lived in

| England | Norway | Iceland | Scotland |

2 What was the name of Eirik Bloodaxe's son, whom Egil had killed?

| Rognvald | Athelstan | Arinbjorn | Eirik |

3 What stopped Egil from concentrating on composing the poem?

| people shouting | a swallow twittering | he was sleepy | a dog barking |

4 What was the name of King Eirik Bloodaxe's wife?

| Gunnhild | Elizabeth | Ethel | Anne |

5 For which king had Egil fought in England?

| Rognvald | Athelstan | Eirik Bloodaxe | Arinbjorn |

6 Whom did Egil plan to visit when he returned to England?

| King Eirik Bloodaxe | King Athelstan | Queen Gunnhild | Arinbjorn |

Reading Test – Fiction

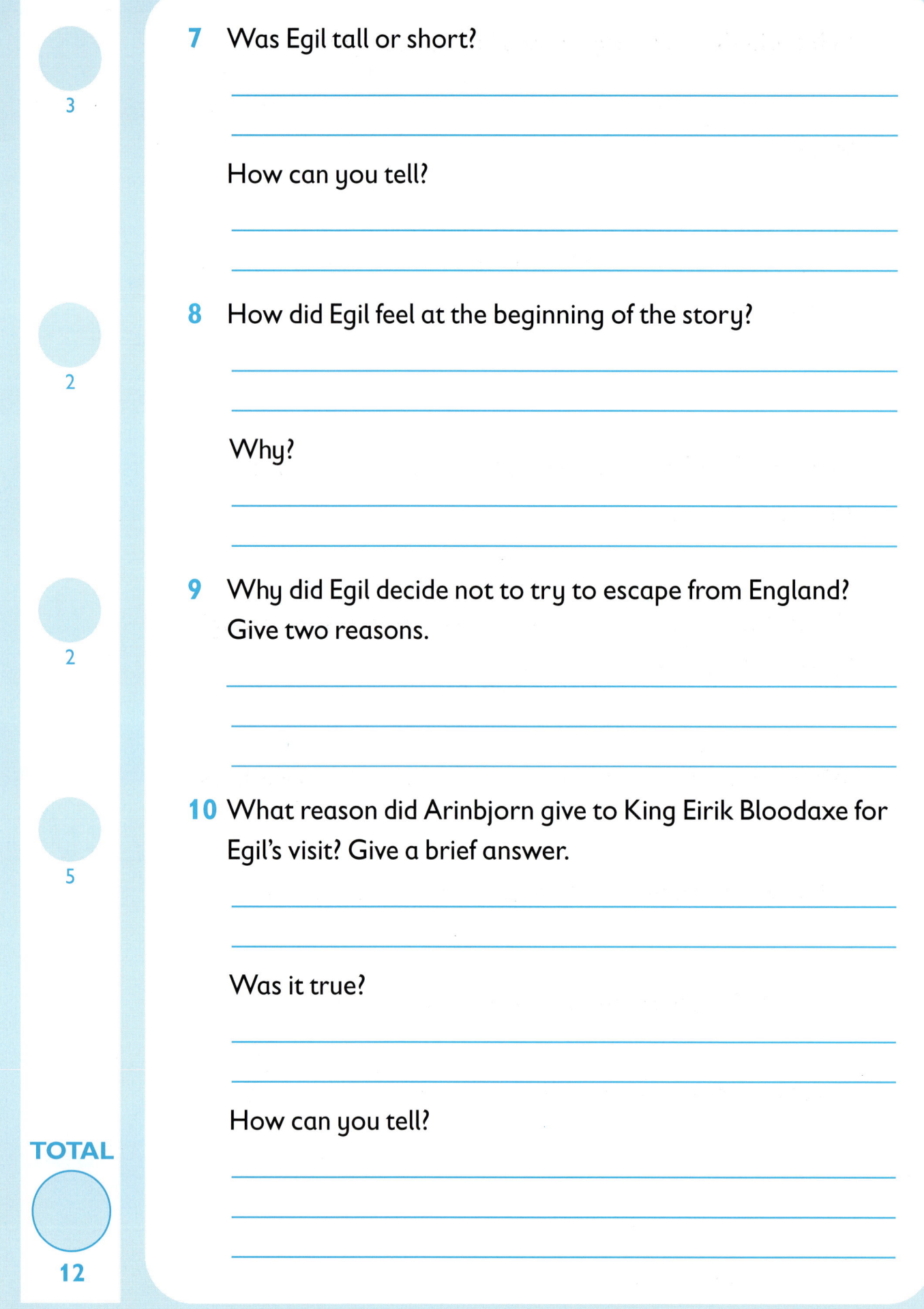

7 Was Egil tall or short?

How can you tell?

8 How did Egil feel at the beginning of the story?

Why?

9 Why did Egil decide not to try to escape from England? Give two reasons.

10 What reason did Arinbjorn give to King Eirik Bloodaxe for Egil's visit? Give a brief answer.

Was it true?

How can you tell?

TOTAL
12

34

Reading Test – Fiction

11 What did King Eirik say should happen to Egil?

Why?

12 What tells you that Arinbjorn thought King Eirik could be persuaded by flattery?

13 Why did King Eirik not kill Egil on the night he went to see him?

14 What shows that King Eirik trusted Arinbjorn, even though he was a friend of Egil?

15 What did Arinbjorn see when he went to look for the swallow?

What do you think it was and who might have sent it?

16 What sort of character do you think Gunnhild was?

Give two examples from the story to support your answer.

2

1

1

1

3

3

TOTAL

11

35

Reading Test – Fiction

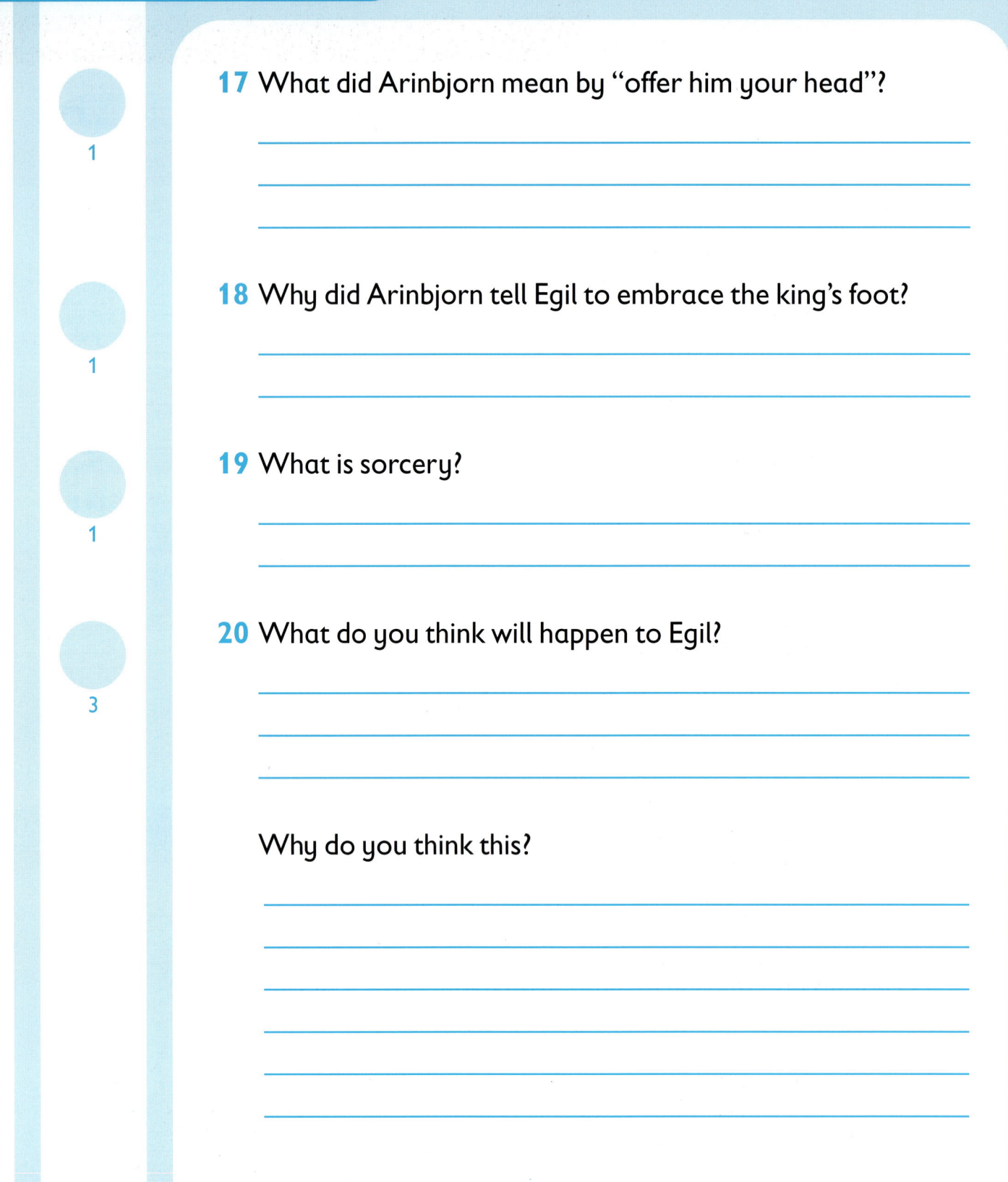

17 What did Arinbjorn mean by "offer him your head"?

_____
_____
_____

18 Why did Arinbjorn tell Egil to embrace the king's foot?

_____
_____

19 What is sorcery?

_____
_____

20 What do you think will happen to Egil?

_____
_____
_____

Why do you think this?

_____
_____
_____
_____
_____

TOTAL 6

Reading Test
Poetry

The Head Ransom
(Egils's poem to King Eirik Bloodaxe)

By sun and moon
I journeyed West,
My sea-borne tune
From Odin's[1] breast,
My song-ship packed
With poet's art:
Its word-keel cracked
The frozen heart.

And now I feed
With an English king:
To English mead[2]
I word-mead bring,
Your praise my task,
My song your fame,
If you but ask
I shall sound your name.

These praises, king,
Will not cost you dear
That I shall sing
If you will hear:
Who beat and blazed
Your trail of red,
Until Odin gazed
Upon the dead.

The scream of swords,
The clash of shields:
These are true words
On battlefields.
Man sees his death
Frozen in dreams,
But Eirik's breath
Frees battle-streams.

[1] Odin: the chief Norse god (and god of war)
[2] Mead: a drink made from honey

37

Reading Test – Poetry

1 In which direction did Egil travel?

| North | South | East | West |

2 What does man see frozen in dreams?

| his future | ghosts | his death | battles |

3 What does Egil mean by 'My song-ship packed/With poet's art'?

| I sailed here specially to deliver this poem. | My ship was full of poets. | I have a singing ship. | We sang all the way here. |

4 What does Egil say his task is?

| to fight battles | to praise the king | to amuse the king | to die a hero |

5 Which two lines in the poem gave you the answer to Question 4?

_____

_____

TOTAL 6

Reading Test – Poetry

6 In which two lines in the poem does Egil say that his poem will make King Eirik treat him kindly?

_____

_____

2

7 What is the atmosphere of this poem?

_____

Give three lines to support your answer.

_____

_____

_____

3

8 Give two examples of kennings in the poem and explain them.

_____

_____

2

TOTAL

7

39

Reading Test
Information

The Jorvik Viking Centre

The Jorvik Viking Centre is unique – once experienced, never forgotten. It is built on the exact site of a huge archaeological dig.

The dig revealed the amazingly well-preserved remains of part of the Viking City of Jorvik from the time of King Eirik Bloodaxe, cocooned in wet mud (and therefore perfectly preserved) for more than 1,000 years. A massive range of detailed, often microscopic, evidence was recovered and has been used to recreate scenes of everyday life. This is no waxworks: this is the closest you'll ever get to time travel – the sights, the sounds and even the very smells of Jorvik in AD 948.

Starting from the moment you arrive at our door, Viking inhabitants of the York of 1,000 years ago will be eager to tell you the best place to buy wooden bowls or bone skates, and tell you about the city in their day, as well as preparing you for your journey back in time. You can dress up as a raider with a sword. Then you descend the stairs to Viking levels – to the level of York's streets as they were in 948 before they were buried beneath the rubbish of subsequent generations.

Climb aboard your magic timecar and then, moving backwards on a journey through time, you will start to move closer and closer to the world of the Vikings in York.

As you emerge from a cordwainer's (shoemaker's) workshop, it is 948 and you are in the bustling market of Coppergate (Coopers' Street) with its mass of traders all shouting for your custom and trying to be heard over all the other noises, of animals, workmen, carts etc. You then turn down one of countless alleys between the houses, workshops and market stalls, and head towards the river. Pick your way past more tradesmen, fighting dogs and scrapping children. You can drive right through a dark, smoky house where a family prepares an evening meal. Herbs, animal skins and furs hang above their heads and foraging chickens cluck around their feet. In the corner children finish spinning and weaving before dinner is ready.

Through the back door and past the squealing piglets, an old chap is sitting on the toilet. Moss and torn-up pieces of old clothes lie on the screen ready for use as toilet paper.

You approach a boat which has just arrived. The sailors sort the cargo, singing songs and cracking a joke or two. Fishermen exchange seafaring yarns, to the delight of a Viking boy who is on fish-gutting duties that evening.

Your journey through time then leaps 1,000 years forwards, as you enter the archaeological excavations upon which the street scene is based. You go through the remains of the house you saw reconstructed.

You leave via the shop, where you can buy books, authentic jewellery and even carved replica bone combs and 'Eirik Bloodaxe rules OK' T-shirts! In the coin-maker's workshop you can strike a Viking coin using copies of the very moulds found on the site.

Reading Test – Information

1 In which city is the Jorvik Viking Centre?

| the text does not say | York | London | Chester |

2 About how long ago was there a Viking settlement at Jorvik?

| a thousand years | a hundred years | a million years | fifty years |

3 What kept the remains of Jorvik in such good condition for all that time?

| smoke | wet mud | pieces of moss | herbs |

4 Which three animals did the people of Jorvik have?

_____

5 Why are the streets of Jorvik much lower than the modern streets?

_____

_____

6 Name five trades or jobs of adults in Jorvik.

_____

_____

1

1

1

3

1

5

TOTAL

12

Reading Test – Information

7 What three jobs did children do?

_____

_____

_____

3

8 Which two words or phrases are used to create the impression of a busy scene in Coppergate?

_____

_____

2

9 How is the Jorvik Centre different from most museums?

_____

_____

1

10 Which three words or phrases are used to impress this difference upon the reader?

_____

_____

_____

3

11 What kind of audience is addressed by the passage?

_____

How can you tell?

_____

_____

2

TOTAL 11

42

Reading Test – Information

12 List any exaggerations or strong adjectives or verbs which are used to show the reader that a visit to the Jorvik Centre will be fun.

_____
_____
_____

3

13 Is the language formal or informal?

_____

5

What is it about the person and the form of the verbs which tells you whether the language is formal or informal?

_____
_____
_____

Copy a sentence with examples of the verb and person which show this. Underline the verb and person.

_____
_____

TOTAL

8

43

Writing Test

This test helps you to gain an insight into your child's ability to write independently: to communicate meaning to the reader using the conventions of punctuation, spelling and handwriting.

The writing test in this book covers the writing of:

- fiction
- information.

> Sheets of lined paper are provided on pages 47 to 48 and 50 to 51 for your child to write on.
>
> Your child should first have read the passages in the Reading Test.
>
> Allow 30 minutes for each part of the test.
>
> There are no definitive answers, but an indication of National Curriculum levels is given on pages 58–60.

Fiction Writing Test

1. Give your child the planning sheet on page 46.
2. Read the starting point aloud.
3. Introduce the planning sheet and discuss the headings on it.

Emphasise the importance of:

- writing a whole story in the letter, not just part of it;
- planning the letter;
- thinking of a good opening to make the reader want to read on;
- keeping the reader interested;
- helping the reader to get to know the characters Egil meets;
- thinking of a good ending, rather than stopping abruptly.

You must not tell your child what to write!

4. Point out that grammar, spelling and punctuation are important.
5. Remind your child to think about punctuation and how it helps the reader to make sense of what is written.
6. If your child finishes the test before 30 minutes are up, encourage him or her to read it through to look for anything which can be improved and to check grammar, spelling and punctuation.

Writing Test

Information Writing Test

1. Give your child the planning sheet (page 49).

2. Read the starting point aloud.

3. Discuss the points on the planning sheet:

   - thinking up a good introduction to make the reader want to read on;
   - keeping the reader interested;
   - making the text easy for the reader to follow;
   - thinking of a good ending so that the information does not just 'tail off'.

   You must not tell your child what to write!

4. Point out that grammar, spelling and punctuation are important.

5. Remind your child to think about punctuation and how it helps the reader to make sense of what is written.

6. If your child finishes the test before 30 minutes are up, encourage him or her to read it through to look for anything which can be improved and to check grammar, spelling and punctuation.

Writing Test
Fiction

Egil's Saga

Read *Egil's Saga* (pages 31 to 32).

Write a letter from Egil to his family at home in Iceland, telling them what happened.

Before you write your letter, you need to plan it.

Make some very brief notes in the spaces below.

- What might have been going through Egil's mind at different points in the story?

- What might he have been thinking about the other characters?

- What words can you use to make the reader want Egil to survive?

- How can you include all the information from the passage?

- What kind of atmosphere do you want to show in the letter, and how will you do that?

Writing Test – Fiction

LEVEL

Writing Test
Information

Read *Egil's Saga*, the poem *The Head Ransom* and the information passage about the Jorvik Centre.

Write a newspaper report describing a visit to the Jorvik Centre.

Plan your writing:

- Think about the purpose of your writing.
  Think about the way in which people read newspapers, and where they read them. How will this affect your writing?
  How will you make it easy for someone reading very quickly to gain an impression of the Jorvik Centre?

- Think of a headline.

- Think of other headings.

- Think about the layout of your writing.

Writing Test – Information

Writing Test – Information

LEVEL

Spelling Test

This test contains words which are generally known by 10 year-olds. They include many of the spelling strategies, rules and conventions suggested for Year 5 and the list of high-frequency words for Year 5 in the National Literacy Strategy *Framework for Teaching*.

> This test is a short passage with words missed out.
>
> Copy the passage on page 61 and underline the words in **bold**. These are the missing words.
>
> Your child writes on the test copy on page 53.
>
> Allow 15 minutes for the Spelling Test.
>
> At the end of the test give a mark for each correct word and enter it in the space provided.
>
> National Curriculum levels are given on page 62.

1. Ask your child to listen to you reading the complete text.

2. Ask your child to look at his or her copy of the text. Point out that some of the words have been left out.

3. Tell your child that you are going to read the text again and that he or she should write in the missing words as you read.

4. Read the text aloud again, pausing after each word in bold type to give your child time to write it on the test copy.

You can repeat each of the bold words up to three times, if necessary.

Egil was _____. He was _____ for _____ sea-voyage. Some years had _____ since his _____ expedition to Norway. There had been a _____ sea-fight off the coast of Norway, and he had killed Rognvald, the son of King Eirik Bloodaxe, and thirteen of his _____. Eirik _____ Egil an outlaw, and his wife, Queen Gunnhild, who was _____ for her sorcery, put a curse on him.

Egil could not go to Norway – he would be _____ at once. But England was _____ safe for him – he had _____ in a _____ _____ on the side of the king of England, Athelstan: the king owed him a _____. So Egil prepared his ship. In the summer, he left his wife, Asgerd, in _____ of their farm at Borg in Iceland, and sailed to England.

He landed on the east coast, not far from York. But he _____ that King Eirik Bloodaxe was there! He had been _____ from Norway and was now king of the Norse _____ in York. Egil realised that he had no _____ of getting away, even in _____. _____ would recognise him.
Besides, he thought it demeaning to be _____ trying to run away. So he _____ himself and made up his mind to go to the king.

Handwriting Test

Handwriting Test

Allow 5 minutes for this test.

1. Read the instructions with your child

2. He or she should copy the passage onto the lines provided.

3. The National Curriculum guidelines on page 62 will help you to judge your child's level in handwriting.

Handwriting Test

Handwriting Test

Copy this passage as neatly as you can onto the lines below it.

Egil was restless. He was ready for another sea-voyage. Some years had passed since his raiding expedition to Norway. There had been a furious sea-fight off the coast of Norway, and he had killed Rognvald, the son of King Eirik Bloodaxe, and thirteen of his friends.

LEVEL

Answers

Reading Test

Fiction Reading Test

Question number	Answer	Mark
1	Iceland	1
2	Rognvald	1
3	a swallow twittering	1
4	Gunnhild	1
5	Athelstan	1
6	King Athelstan	1
7	Tall. King Eirik could see him above the other men. 'Towering figure'	3 *(1 mark for each)*
8	Restless. He had not been on a sea-voyage for a long time.	2 *(1 mark for each)*
9	He thought he would be recognised and caught. He would be ashamed to be caught running away.	2 *(1 mark for each)*
10	He said that Egil had sailed to England specially to be reconciled with Eirik Bloodaxe. It was not true. Egil planned to visit King Athelstan. He did not know that Eirik Bloodaxe was there, and he wanted to get away from York when he heard that Eirik was there.	2 1 2
11	He should be killed. Just one of the things he had done was bad enough for him to deserve to die.	2 *(1 mark for each)*
12	Arinbjorn tried to persuade him to let Egil live by saying that he would compose 'a poem of praise which will live for ever'.	1
13	It was shameful to kill someone at night.	1
14	He let him take Egil back to his home.	1
15	A strange shape. Something magic *or* something ghostly It might have been sent by Gunnhild.	3 1 mark for mentioning Gunnhild
16	Evil. She was known for her sorcery. She urged King Eirik to kill Egil.	3 *(1 mark for each)*
17	Say that you are giving yourself up to the king's mercy.	1
18	To show humility/that the king was a great man.	1
19	Witchcraft/casting spells/magic.	1
20	Any answer which is justified by reference to the passage.	3

Poetry Reading Test

Question number	Answer	Mark
1	West	1
2	his death	1
3	I sailed here specially to deliver this poem	1
4	To praise the king	1
5	Your praise my task/My song your fame	2 *(1 mark for each)*
6	Its word-keel cracked/The frozen heart	2 *(1 mark for each)*
7	Warlike. Any three from: Who beat and blazed. Your trail of red. The scream of swords. The clash of shields. On battlefields. Frees battle-streams. The god of war.	3 *(1 mark for each line, maximum 3 marks)*
8	Any two from: Song-ship. Word-keel. Word-mead. Any meanings which the child can justify.	2 A kenning is a compound (two-part) expression.

Information Reading Test

Question number	Answer	Mark
1	York	1
2	a thousand years	1
3	wet mud	1
4	Dogs, pigs and chickens.	3 *(1 mark each)*
5	Rubbish has piled up on them over the centuries.	1
6	Fisherman, sailor, shoemaker/cordwainer, cooper, coin-maker.	5 *(1 mark for each)*
7	Spinning, weaving, fish-gutting.	3 *(1 mark for each)*
8	Bustling. Mass of traders.	2
9	It is built on the exact site of an archaeological dig.	1
10	Unique. Once experienced, never forgotten. This is no waxworks.	3
11	Children *or* families. You can dress up as a raider with a sword. Magic timecar.	2
12	Unique, huge, massive, microscopic, intricate, eager, descend, magic, bustling, countless, scrapping, squealing etc.	3
13	Informal. The verbs are active and most of it is in the second person. *Any sentence with an active verb in the second person, for example* 'You can dress up as a raider'.	5

Answers
Writing Test

There are three aspects to consider in your child's achievement in writing:

1. Organisation and purpose (the content of the story or, in information writing, the form and content of the text).

2. Grammar (the correct use of punctuation, capital letters, tenses and pronouns).

3. Style (use of connective words, sentence structure and vocabulary).

Your child might do better in one of these aspects than in the others. Looking at his or her writing in this way helps to pinpoint strengths and weaknesses.

The following descriptions will help you to gain an idea of your child's level in writing.

ORGANISATION AND PURPOSE
Fiction writing

Level 3	Level 4	Level 5
• The main features of letter-writing are used appropriately: sender's address, date and a suitable ending. • The child has thought about the structure of the story and does not just list one event after another. • Some description is given of the places to which Egil went and the people he met. • The child has made an attempt to convey Egil's feelings.	• The child has used paragraphs to separate the beginning, middle (or the events which take place) and the ending. • The events are linked in a logical way. • The characters respond to one another's words and actions. The characters develop as the letter progresses.	• There is a good structure and the child shows a good grasp of the narrative form. Dialogue is mixed with events and description. • The reader's interest is kept through the use of techniques such as dialogue and change of place or time. The child makes comments on what is happening and indicates the thoughts or feelings of characters. • The opening, main events and ending are divided by paragraphs.

Writing Test Answers

Information Writing

Level 3	Level 4	Level 5
• As well as a headline, sub-headings are used. • There is a sentence of introduction. • Some connection is made between the points. • There is an attempt at explanation.	• There is a headline. • Sub-headings are carefully sequenced to give an 'at-a-glance' overview of the report. Some paragraphs are used within the sections. • There is an introduction. • Points are sequenced with care. • There is a conclusion (the writing does not end as if the writer has just decided to stop). • All the information a reader needs is included.	• The child uses layout, sub-headings and other appropriate conventions competently. • The text is tailored to the reader (for example, by an introduction to engage interest and to set out the purpose of the report). • Points made are linked and set out in a logical order, and there is a suitable conclusion (for example, a summary). • The report is well structured and presents a point of view.

GRAMMAR

Level 3	Level 4	Level 5
• At least half of the sentences on the first page start with a capital letter and finish with a full stop or question mark or exclamation mark.	• At least three-quarters of the sentences on the first page start with a capital letter and finish with a full stop, question mark, or exclamation mark. • Commas are used to separate parts of a sentence or items in a list. • The tense is consistent – either the past or present. • Quotation marks are used to show where direct speech begins and ends in at least half the instances. • Pronouns are consistent: for example, there is no sudden change from 'you' to 'they'.	• There are few sentences without the correct use of capital letters and full stops, exclamation marks or question marks. Capital letters are used to begin proper nouns. • Commas, speech marks, dashes and brackets are used appropriately.

59

Writing Test Answers

STYLE		
Fiction		
Level 3	**Level 4**	**Level 5**
• The sentence structures are more like those of written than spoken language. • Connectives are used to show contrast, to connect time and for explanation: 'but', 'when', 'also', 'so', 'because'.	• The style is different from spoken language: it has the form of written language. • More complex connectives are used: 'when', 'although', 'if', 'in the meantime'. • Interesting words and phrases make the writing more effective: 'shaking with fear', 'with a scared look'.	• Both simple and complex sentences are used appropriately. • Imaginative vocabulary is used. The child conveys meaning through precise use of language. • The child makes appropriate choices about the use of standard or non-standard English, including dialogue words and colloquial expressions.

Information		
Level 3	**Level 4**	**Level 5**
• The sentence structures are more like those of written than spoken language. • Connectives are used to show contrast, to connect time and for explanation: 'but', 'when', 'also', 'so', 'because'. • Vocabulary includes words such as 'slightly', 'respect', 'honour'.	• The style is different from spoken language: it has the form of written language. • More complex connectives are used: 'when', 'although', 'if', 'in the meantime'. • Interesting words and phrases make the writing more effective: 'people were queuing to buy T-shirts with modern words of praise for Eirik Bloodaxe – Eirik Bloodaxe Rules OK', 'we travelled backwards through time'.	• More than one type of sentence structure and length is used to add interest. • The child can use both active and passive verbs (for example 'you can do something about it'/'something can be done about it'). • Repetition is avoided by the use of words such as 'it', 'they', 'which'. • Subject-specific words such as 'cordwainer' and 'archaeologist' are used. • The child can judge whether or not the tone of the writing should be formal or informal.

Answers
Spelling Test

Egil was **restless**. He was **ready** for **another** sea-voyage. Some years had **passed** since his **raiding** expedition to Norway. There had been a **furious** sea-fight off the coast of Norway, and he had killed Rognvald, the son of King Eirik Bloodaxe, and thirteen of his **friends**. Eirik **declared** Egil an outlaw, and his wife, Queen Gunnhild, who was **known** for her sorcery, put a curse on him.

Egil could not go to Norway – he would be **killed** at once. But England was **surely** safe for him – he had **fought** in a **great battle** on the side of the king of England, Athelstan: the king owed him a **favour**. So Egil prepared his ship. In the summer, he left his wife, Asgerd, in **charge** of their farm at Borg in Iceland, and sailed to England.

He landed on the east coast, not far from York. But he **discovered** that King Eirik Bloodaxe was there! He had been **expelled** from Norway and was now king of the Norse **people** in York. Egil realised that he had no **chance** of getting away, even in **disguise**. **Someone** would recognise him. Besides, he thought it demeaning to be **caught** trying to run away. So he **steeled** himself and made up his mind to go to the king.

Award 1 mark per correct spelling.

National Curriculum Levels

Use the conversion tables below to gain an idea of your child's National Curriculum level from his or her test marks in Reading and Spelling. For Writing, see the National Curriculum level charts on pages 58 to 60.

Fiction Reading	
Mark	**Level**
0 – 7	Below Level 2
8 – 14	Level 2
15 – 24	Level 3
25 – 32	Level 4
33 – 35	Approaching Level 5

Information Reading	
Mark	**Level**
0 – 5	Below Level 2
6 – 11	Level 2
12 – 21	Level 3
22 – 28	Level 4
29 – 31	Approaching Level 5

Poetry Reading	
0 – 2	Below Level 2
3 – 6	Level 2
7 – 9	Level 3
10 – 11	Level 4
12 – 13	Approaching Level 5

Spelling	
0 – 3	Below Level 2
4 – 12	Level 2
13 – 17	Level 3
18 – 21	Level 4
22 – 24	Approaching Level 5

Handwriting	
Indications	**Level**
Legible, but letters are irregular	Below Level 2
Most letters are written correctly. Upper and lower cases are used properly.	Level 2
All letters are written accurately and the writing is controlled.	Level 3
Letters are joined and legible. Ascenders (upstrokes) and descenders (downstrokes) are the correct size.	Level 4
Joined, clear, legible and fluent.	Level 5